SEVEN POWERFUL

Steps to Happiness

SEVEN POWERFUL *Steps to Happiness*

Keys to Victorious Living

ROXANNE EILERS

ISBN: 978-1-7923-5276-8

DEDICATION

THIS BOOK IS dedicated to all of my brothers and sisters in Christ who are struggling to live a victorious life in Christ. We struggle together. We experience victories together. We grow together as we learn God's truths and apply them to our lives. We are all one Body in Christ, the Beloved of God, chosen and set apart for His use and glory.

This book is also dedicated to all those who are seeking happiness and perhaps are not Christian. May God open our hearts to hear His Word and allow it to change our thinking, thus changing our lives forever.

TABLE OF CONTENTS

INTRODUCTION

*T*HIS BOOK IS down to earth and written for everyone who would like to experience a fuller and more satisfying life. If you follow the steps in this book you are well on your way to increasing happiness in your life. I am not saying it will be easy or you will not encounter difficulty, grief, suffering and trial, for this is part of being human. What I am saying is that in the middle of all the stuff you can *choose* to be happy. You can teach yourself to be content in whatever circumstance you are facing right now. I did not say it is smooth going or without effort to choose happiness, but it is your best option in this life.

What is happiness? Happiness is having a state of well being and contentment even when times or circumstances are unfavorable. I believe we can be happy and that's why I wrote this book. It starts in your heart, your mind and your thoughts. Happiness is an attitude that you can cultivate in your life; cultivating a happy attitude will help diminish emotional pain and hopelessness. It is important to keep hope alive in our hearts because with hope comes a sense of purpose and with purpose comes a feeling of well being. Just knowing there is a purpose for everything that happens in our lives brings some direction amidst the helter skelter.

Of course, there are other ways of encouraging one to be happy, but I found that these seven steps are what helped transform my own heart and life. I believe following these seven steps to happiness will revolutionize your heart and life and will aid you on your journey in life. I like to think of this little book as a handbook for happiness. Don't skip any step because they all work together.

Now I would like to address those who are struggling with depression and mental illness, and those going through deep emotional suffering and grief. I have been there and I know how difficult it is to feel happiness and joy. I suffered a complete mental breakdown when I was seventeen and battled with dark depression and mental illness for many years. Later in my early sixties, I lost our only child by a car accident. He was 22 years old. What helped me through those trying times were these seven steps, plus psychotherapy, (counseling) medication when I needed it, and prayer. There is a place where God wants to take you where you can be happy even while working on your personal issues. I know; I've been there and God is continually beckoning me to live with Him there especially during rough seasons in my life.

Change does not happen overnight but as we are persistent and purpose in our hearts to be happy, gradually new positive thought patterns will emerge and feelings of well-being. If at times you feel like giving up, don't you dare! Life is too good and you need to come through to the other side of pain. Always come through to the other side. This is completing a cycle of suffering no matter how long it takes. With God's help and strength and your determination, you can be happy!

1

BELIEVE IN GOD

I N THIS WORLD, life can get really complicated and at times we don't know if we are coming or going. Before I found God or I should say He found me, my life was chaotic and out of control. As an adolescent, I felt so lost and without hope. The world seemed like a dangerous place to me. It was so big and I felt so small—I just wanted to find a safe place to hide and get my thoughts together, to try and make some sense out of the life I was living. I spoke to many people about life and its purpose. I spoke about death. I spoke about God. Was there a God? One of my good friends did not think so, and he told me that he didn't believe. He said that when I died that would be the end of me. I could not accept this. This idea horrified me—to cease to exist? This threw my confused thoughts and emotions into a tail spin. If I just ceased to exist, what reason did I have living in this world? I was without God and without hope in the world. I had no real purpose.

Things got worse for me as I wrestled my way through fear, guilt and hopelessness. Finally all the stress I was under at home and at school took its toll on me emotionally. At seventeen, a senior in high school, I suffered a mental breakdown. Now I really had something to worry about—my broken mind and splintered emotions. Where is God I screamed! Is there a God? What is the purpose of this life? I desperately needed answers.

Two weeks after the breakdown God made Himself known to me. The Bible says if you search and seek for God with all of your heart, He will be found by you (Jeremiah 29:13). I went in to see one of my counselors and told him I felt out of touch with reality. At the time I didn't even know that what had happened to me was a breakdown. All I knew was that I was in a state of continuous panic, terror, guilt and tremendous confusion of thoughts. I had become mentally ill and my life as I knew it was no longer there. I was different inside. It was as if I was a glass that had been thrown down and shattered into a thousand pieces. How could I put it all together again? I talked to my counselor and he asked me if I would like to talk to a friend of his. I said yes. I would speak to anyone who could help me.

So the next day I waited with my little dog, Boston, out front on the high school campus to speak to this lady. As she walked up I had some hope rise in my heart. She sat with me and I poured out my heart to her. Then she began to share with me about God. Talk about an answer to my searching—God revealed Himself to me through this woman and through what she said to me.

She told me that the Bible said that God loved me and had a plan for my life. God knew me personally and had called me to Himself. But I was separated from God because of my sins. What is sin? Sin is when we go our own way instead of God's way. It is breaking His laws. Yes, I had sinned. The Bible says that the wages of sin is death, this is spiritual death (Romans 6:23). But then she went on to say that God already took care of the payment for my sin and the sins of the whole world, and that was through the death of His only Son, Jesus Christ. God loved the world so much that He did something that would take care of the sin problem forever. He gave His only Son, that whosoever believes in Him will not perish but have everlasting life (John 3:16).

This wonderful woman told me that Jesus Christ came into our world, took on human flesh and showed us what God the Father is like. Jesus was nailed to the cross for our sins; He was buried and rose again from the dead the third day. He is alive and in heaven waiting for people on earth to believe on Him and to receive forgiveness for their sins. He wants to give us the gift of God which is *eternal life* in Christ—that means living forever with Him. He also wants to give us the Holy Spirit to live in us and be with us as we live our lives, preparing us for the next life.

This was extremely good news for my weary heart of despair. Something clicked inside of me and I knew this was all true. God was real. Jesus was real. When I died it wasn't the end. I wasn't just dead as a dog. Hope rose in my heart. I had a purpose in this life. I wanted God's plan for my life. I wanted God. I wanted to give my life to Him and live for Him for the rest of my life. This beautiful woman led me in a prayer to receive God's gift of Jesus and eternal life. It went something like this:

Dear Heavenly Father, I believe You love me and that Jesus died on the cross for my sins. I believe He was buried and rose again from the dead. I ask You to forgive me for breaking Your laws and going my own way. Now I ask You to come and live in my heart and make me Your own. Show me the plan You have for my life. Thank You so much, I pray this in the name of Your Son, Jesus Christ. Amen.

So I cried and cried and prayed and cried some more. All I knew was that my life had changed again and this time in a wonderful way. Although my emotions were still confused and fear reigned in my mind, I hung on to the hope that Jesus would somehow, some way help me through all this pain and make me better. This was the first day of being born again into the Kingdom of God.

As the years went on I got married to a very special man, Ike, and had a precious son, Joseph. God blessed me in so many ways and continued to reveal Himself to me as I walked with Him. One of the main ways He revealed Himself was through His Word, the Bible. Over the years He has brought me through my suffering and terrible pain. But this is another whole story in itself. You can read more about my life and how I learned to hold on to hope in a difficult and challenging season in my book, *Hope in a Season of Suffering*.

So the first step is to put your faith in God—the true God of the Bible. I have found this first step of believing in God to be vital for happiness. It is not just believing in *a* God, but it is believing in *the* God and in His only Son, Jesus Christ. It is not just head knowledge of knowing there is a God, but it is choosing to believe in your heart that Jesus paid the price for your sin and that believing in Him you have eternal life. The Bible says we actually pass from death unto life when we believe and place our trust in Him. The Greek word for "believe" is *pistis* which means "placing complete confidence in, trusting one's self to." It is putting all your confidence and trust in Him. It is following Him. In the book of Hebrews 11:6 we are told that the person who comes to God must believe that He exists and that He is a *"rewarder of those who diligently seek Him."* God invites us to go beyond just believing He exists though. God asks us to seek Him with all our hearts to get to know His love and care for us. That word "seek" in the Greek is *ekzeteo* which means "search out, seek after, crave, seek out for one's self." God says if you seek for Him with all your heart you will be rewarded. God rewards us with salvation, forgiveness, peace of heart and mind, spiritual blessings, answered prayer, His presence, power, and knowing Him, just to name a few of His blessings.

If you are not sure about God, just ask Him to make Himself real to you as I did, and if you would like to, pray that same prayer I did and let your new life begin today. God meant for us to have hope and a future not only in this life but also in the next. Eternity is built into our hearts—we want to live forever. Our own hearts tell us there is more after this life.

God has made Himself known to mankind through His beautiful, awesome creation and through His Son. The fullness of the Godhead dwells bodily in the person of Jesus Christ. We need only to take that first step. This first step will revolutionize your entire way of life and thinking. Having faith in God will see you through the most troublesome and trying times in your life. He is our secure Rock that we can turn to again and again for help. He will also help us to implement the other steps to happiness in our lives. He wants us to be happy. Getting to know Him and His person brings peace, joy and happiness in itself. You will want to attend a Bible teaching church and study the Bible yourself. This will help you to grow in your new faith. **Remember: The more we know God intimately, the happier our hearts become.**

Believing in God brings hope into our lives and where there is hope there is strength to go on. If you have secured the first step, then let us go on now to the next step and that is to *live in the present*.

2

LIVE IN THE PRESENT

HAT ARE SOME of the reasons why we don't live in our present? It is hard to live in the present when you are hurting and when you are waiting for something. We may have had better days in the past, or perhaps we are looking to the future to bring us better days. What a huge concept it is to learn to live in the present. I have had to learn this lesson the hard way, and I am still learning it. It will be a lifelong process. All we have is today, our present time that we live in. We have memories of the past, but they are just those, memories. Then we have dreams and visions for our future, or worries and fears about our future, but it is just that, our future that we cannot know or see in the present. You may find that your present is not where you want to be right now. I know exactly what you are feeling. Many times I didn't want to live in my present because it was much too painful. However, over the years God has been teaching me how to live in my present, and when I do I find it a satisfying way to live. So how do we do this?

When I was struggling with major depression, phobias and other problems I found it incredibly difficult to stay in my present. I was so busy worrying about tomorrow's troubles, which in my sensitized mind were magnified. I feared what could happen or might have happened in the past which could ruin my present. I lived with irrational fears along with unreasonable guilt which plagued me from the moment I went to sleep to the moment I arose in the morning. I feared disease, war, violence, dying, getting hurt, hurting others, just to name a few. When would all this emotional upheaval ever end? I didn't know how to live in my present—the concept of time seemed warped and confusing to me.

As time went on I began to try and focus on what I was doing in the present—all the while in the back of my mind fears were brewing, but at least I could keep them in the background. This was a learning process that took time. I would like to say here that it doesn't have to take years to reap some positive results of living in the present if you choose to seriously work on it. It wasn't until I read books and learned from others about living in my present that I really began to understand and practice it.

I remember when I was first learning about this

concept. I read the book *The Precious Present* by Spencer Johnson. So often we are searching and looking everywhere for contentment and fulfillment when it is right there before us each moment in our present—right under our noses. In my therapy sessions I learned that I am not asked to live in the past or future, but just in my present. I learned the Bible also talked about this concept.

It says in Matthew 6:34 that we are not to worry about tomorrow, for tomorrow will worry about itself. 2 Corinthians 12:9 tells us that God's strength is sufficient for all our needs. Philippians 4:13 says that I can do all things through Christ Jesus who gives me strength. This tells me that I can live in my present, and I will have enough strength to deal with it. A favorite Bible verse of mine is Deuteronomy 33:25, *"As your days so shall your strength be."* I live by this verse. This means to me that as my days are so will strength be given. How are our days? They are one at a time, one second at a time, one minute at a time, one hour at a time, one day at a time. I found that I could stand anything for a minute or an hour. I could endure anything for a period of time. So it happened that when I began to feel overwhelmed I would say to myself, "I can stand this discomfort one moment at a time. I will feel better." And I could and did stand it.

I remember when I was in labor and delivery with my

son. I said those words to myself. "I can stand this. I have grace for this moment. I can feel all I can in this moment and not be afraid." And I did make it through without any medication for the pain. It was a natural childbirth! (I'd like to note here that there is nothing wrong with needing medication. I am not insinuating that here. I am saying that living in my present helped me get through the pain of childbirth.)

I found that this mindset worked with anything I found difficult to go through. When my mother-in-law came to live with us it was extremely challenging for me. It was a time of learning many difficult lessons. There were moments that I felt so overwhelmed I thought I would come unglued. I would go up to the hills by our house and I would cry out to God for strength. I would calm myself by pulling myself back into the present. I would think about what was going on right then and there. Sometimes I would breathe in the air or just watch the birds flying overhead. I would sing to the Lord. I would cry. I felt the moment—it was difficult and it hurt, but I felt it and then I moved on to facing my situation back home. I would purposely be conscious of what I was doing as I brought myself back to live and stay in my present.

I can still remember when my sister was dying of breast cancer and I was flying out to see her. I worried and wondered how I could handle this along with all the other fears and personal struggles I was experiencing? I prayed and I remembered the Scriptures that said I would have enough strength for my day. So I boarded the jet with much anxiety, but I could stand what I needed to stand for a higher gain, that of seeing my sister for the last time and comforting her family. Throughout the plane flight I focused on my present. I told myself God was with me and I would be okay. I also directed my thoughts on what God would have me do when I saw my sister. As I arrived and stayed at my sister's house God gave me sufficient grace and strength for each moment. Was it easy to live in my present? No. I had moments of panic. Moments of fear and weakness, but I determined to do God's will and to make it through each moment—each hour. God honored my choosing to do good.

Remember that we can think about the past and the future, but we must not live there in fear or worry. We can plan and dream and reminisce old times, but we are not made to live there—we are made to live fully in our present and to enjoy, feel, and experience all that is in our present. Sometimes we will feel sad, lonely, distressed; other times we will feel joyful, happy and carefree. Remember that you can make it through uncomfortable feelings—they will not overtake you. Trust God with your present, your past and your future.

There was another time when so much was going on

in my life. Ike and I had moved up to Orange County to work on our Masters in Theological Studies. Our son, Joseph was with us and Ike's elderly mother still lived with us. I was in school and it was finals week. I was taking Greek and another full-time class. My father was dying with cancer in the hospital and my mother was just being placed in an assisted living facility. We were in the middle of moving to another apartment, and financially we were broke. I began to panic when I thought of all these things going on in my life—how could I make it? What if I break under all this pressure? How can I handle Daddy's death? How can I stand all this stuff? I had so many questions.

Then I could faintly hear God speaking to me in the middle of all my overwhelming thoughts. I could hear Him saying, "Take no thought for tomorrow." Oh yes! Then I remembered. I can make it through this time by living in my present. God promises strength and grace in my present. So I drew myself back to the moment where I was presently going for a walk. I breathed in the fresh air and smelled the fragrant flowers along the way. I knew I could make it and would make it through each moment, each hour, and the next day. And so this is how I lived. It worked! I made it through that extremely difficult time.

The greatest testing of what I have learned about this concept came however, when we lost our only child. He was hit by a car while crossing the street. At 22 years old he was gone in an instant. Our lives were abruptly changed and things came to a screeching halt. As I look back on those days I remember of constantly having to pull myself back into the moment leaning into the arms of Jesus, allowing Him to carry me. When the pain became too great and I began to panic, I prayed and recited the truth to myself. The truth was that this too would all pass. Others made it through and I would also. God will never give me more than I can stand up under. I gradually regained my center as I walked through each moment with Him. Each day was a "one step at a time" day. Each day my goal was to make it through to the end of that day until I laid my head down on my pillow that night. It was not an easy task to stay in my present when the pain was so draining, however, it was doing just this that helped bring me into the healing of my loss. During these tremendously challenging times everything I believed in that I thought would help me was tried and tested to the limit. God never failed. The other steps I will be talking about, including living in the present, also were anchors for me. For them to work though, I had to determine to put them into practice religiously. There were times I was stuck in the past memories of my life with my son. During these times I allowed myself to reminisce these memories and then slowly I pulled myself back into the present. I had to be there for those who were still with me on this earth. Eventually over the weeks, months and years my sorrow began to be turned into a peaceful acceptance of what was.

Living in the present can work for you too. It takes practice, but with practice it can become a part of you so that you just naturally go back to that way of thinking and living every time you find yourself getting stuck in the past or the future. Here I would like to add that living in the present not only gives us victory through our unpleasant moments, but also we can enjoy life more fully by savoring the happy moments.

If you are with your spouse, be in that moment, really look into each other's eyes; take their hand in yours. If you are with your children, be in that moment, laugh and make the time fun together. If you are eating dinner, enjoy your food, savor the flavors. If you are watching a good movie or riding a bike, be in that moment. If you are visiting with a friend, yes, be in that moment—really taste that rich hot coffee.

I would like to add here that when there are not only problems that we are groping with, but also troubles going on around us and in our country, we must still take the same approach. Do what is set before you to do. Line upon line. Here a little, there a little until you complete your tasks. Try not to let your thoughts wander into the future and allow fear to grab hold of your present. **Remember, guide your thoughts back to the present moment.**

Right now presently I am typing this story for you and I am enjoying it. I am here with you. You get the picture. Remember with God's help you can live in the present. Our next step is to *freely forgive.*

3

FREELY FORGIVE

*O*N MY BOOK, *Faith that Pleases God*, there is a section where I talk about unforgiveness and how it can hinder our faith. Not only can it hinder our faith it can create within us a bitter spirit and a hardness about us. Whenever we get hurt in some way by someone we tend to get angry at them and develop feelings of animosity toward them. They owed it to us to treat us better, or to believe in us, or to give us what we deserved. The list can go on and on with what others owe us.

If we don't forgive the one who hurt us then the next step is we begin to hold a grudge against them. We will find that every time their face pops into our thoughts, negative feelings will arise in our hearts. This feeling of unforgiveness and dislike for this person is really only hurting ourselves because we are the ones who keep thinking about the hurt and licking our wounds.

There are reasons why God has called us to be

forgivers of men. I believe a big reason is because God, in Christ, forgave us of our debts, and He wants us to do as He does—to forgive others their debts. Another reason is because it hurts us emotionally, spiritually and physically. The Bible also tells us that if we carry unforgiveness in our hearts this gives place for the devil to get into our life (2 Corinthians 2:11). The enemy thrives on bitterness and resentment. If we give place to the devil then he can mess with our peace of mind and take away our joy.

I believe it is possible to forgive even those who have wounded us deeply. We can do this because God says we can. Phil. 4:13 says, *"I can do all things through Christ who strengthens me."* This tells me I can forgive if I want to. I believe what happens when we get hurt by someone is that our pride also gets wounded and somewhere inside of us, after we experience these hurt feelings, our initial reaction is that we don't want to forgive. Somehow we would like them to suffer a little.

I remember when I was hurt very deeply by some people from my church denomination. My first reaction was hurt. I felt so bad. They owed it to me to take me under their wing and encourage me and to believe in my abilities in ministry. However, I felt tossed aside and not accepted—I felt like I was not liked or appreciated. After I cried many tears, I began to feel the emotions of anger and dislike for them. I had thoughts that were not pleasing to God. A part of me wanted to see them suffer in some way as I had, then they would understand my situation. It wasn't until I mentioned it to my therapist in my session with her that I really began to work on my feelings.

So what could I do in order to really forgive someone who had done me wrong in some way? We began to look at the incident from different perspectives. This helped some and I began to give them the benefit of the doubt. I thought maybe they just didn't know how to respond to me and my circumstances at the time. Maybe they were going through a difficult season themselves.

It is always good to confide in a close friend or someone you can trust when forgiveness is involved. Perhaps they can help you see it in a different light— a more balanced perception. My therapist then proceeded to give me a prescription on how to forgive.

She told me to get a piece of paper and to write down the name of the person who I needed to forgive. She said to put on one side of the paper, *debts*. Then she asked me to write down all the debts I felt that person owed me. So I did. I wrote down that he owed me encouragement; he owed to give me words of wisdom about my situation. He owed to give me a sense of belonging and a place in the Body of Christ where I could serve in his local church. These were just some of the debts I wrote down. Then she told me to take each one to the

Lord, tell Him about it, and then to draw a line through each of them writing cancelled across it. I did this until there was nothing left that he owed me. I chose to forgive him as Christ had forgiven me for all my debts. I meditated on the fact that Jesus freely crossed out and cancelled all my debts and declared me free from them, holding nothing against me.

I have found that one of the secrets to cultivating a forgiving heart is to pray for that person who offended you. When you pray for her or him something happens within your own heart. A transformation takes place and the bitterness, anger and payback begin to dissipate. If those feelings of hurt and unforgiveness resurface again take them back to Jesus and remind yourself that you cancelled that debt. Ask for Him to heal your troubled emotions and feelings. We must let them off the hook so our hearts can be happy.

It is so vital that our hearts remain tender and gentle to the leading of the Lord, so when we are offended we can freely and quickly forgive and then move on. I understand that there are some things that have been done to us and we have experienced that can be so painful that we feel we just can't forgive because we cannot forget. These incidents may need extra tender care, such as counseling, inner healing with prayer, and therapy. Our goal is to forgive and sometimes it takes time to get there and to be ready to do this. **Remember** that forgiving someone doesn't mean we have to hang out with them or be with them. Sometimes it is best to go our separate ways and for us to guard our hearts from further pain.

One of the hardest people to forgive can be ourselves. I know in my own life I struggled with feelings of self-hate for the wrong choices I had made earlier in my life. It took time, talking about it with my therapist and with God. It took reading books on self-forgiveness, and more self-understanding and strength from God for me to finally forgive and embrace that part of me that I wanted to throw out and forget about. But I accepted myself and my weaknesses and as Christ forgave me completely I forgave myself and grew to love and respect myself. I remembered the verse in the Bible that said, *"Love your neighbor as yourself."*(Leviticus 19:18) If I could love myself, I could love my neighbor also.

Freely forgive. Make it a way of life for you and you will have a lighter and happier heart. God intended it this way. Now the fourth step to happiness we will look at is to *be thankful.*

4

BE THANKFUL

NDER THE HEADING of being thankful I always see the words, *grateful* and *content*. So let us look at being thankful as also including these other two attitudes. How different having a thankful heart can make in a trying situation. When we cultivate a thankful heart our emotions can go from overwhelming frustration, fear, loneliness and hopelessness to peace, confidence and trust. How does this happen? Perhaps as we travel through this chapter we will find out.

The Apostle Paul talks about being thankful many times in the New Testament. Let us look at some of these Scriptures. Ephesians 5: 18-20 tells us to be filled with the Holy Spirit, speaking to each other with psalms, hymns, and *songs* from the Spirit. We are to *sing and make music* from our hearts to the Lord and *always to give thanks to God the Father for everything* in the name of our Lord Jesus Christ. Notice that it is the praise, singing and thanksgiving from our hearts that work together forming an attitude of contentment and gratefulness.

When we are filled with the Spirit of God and we nurture a heart of thanksgiving, and as we worship and praise Him singing songs that are uplifting, it becomes easier to have a grateful heart and to have peace in the midst of whatever is going on.

I would like to interject here something to **remember: I think a huge key thought for being thankful is that if we really believe that God knows what we are going through; He is with us in it, and He will give us the strength to make it through, we can be thankful for the sufferings we may encounter.** I am not saying that we are to be thankful for bad things or evil things that happen, but we are to be thankful for the positive and good that God can bring out of them. We are to be thankful that God is sovereign over all and rules over all things, all situations and all circumstances. We may not understand, but we can trust in God's goodness, mercy, love, wisdom and faithfulness.

When the Apostle Paul was put into prison he focused in on the benefits that could be sifted out of his plight. In the book of Philippians, which is one of his epistles written from prison, chapter 1:12-14 he says, *"Now I want you to know brothers and sisters, that what has happened to me has actually served to advance the gospel. As a result, it has become clear throughout the whole palace guard and to everyone else that I am in chains for Christ. And because of my chains, most of the brothers and sisters have become confident in the Lord and dare all the more to proclaim the gospel without fear.*" Paul was not rejoicing over the horrible conditions in prison, but he saw that his circumstance would bring blessing to some and the gospel was being advanced. His heart rejoiced in God and who He was and that He had control of his life and if He so desired, He would deliver him. This brought a sense of contentment for Paul. He did not write that he could be more effective if God took him out of prison. He had to *learn* not to be in a hurry to get through his time in prison even though it was very uncomfortable. He knew that God would not allow him to be tempted above which he was able but would give him all he needed to make it through—to endure (1 Corinthians 10:13).

Again, in Philippians, chapter four, Paul tells his followers to rejoice in the Lord always. He then says it again—"*Rejoice in the Lord.*" Then he reminds them that they can rejoice because the Lord is near; He is with them in their trials—He understands what they are experiencing and He will always give them strength to make it through and to stay strong in their faith.

Paul says not to be anxious about anything but to pray about everything and then to be thankful. He tells the Christians that if they do this they will experience the peace of God that will guard their hearts and minds.

I believe that Paul struggled with anxious feelings and perhaps feelings of depression in prison because he was a human being just as we are. However, he had to learn to pray instead of worry and to praise and thank God instead of doubt and fear. He says later in that same chapter some powerful words that we can seriously take to heart. He says, *"I am not saying this because I am in need, for I have learned to be content whatever the circumstances. I know what it is to be in need, and I know what it is to have plenty. I have learned the secret of being content in any and every situation, whether well fed or hungry, whether living in plenty or in want. I can do all this through Him who gives me strength.".* Paul had to choose how he was going to respond to his sufferings. With the Holy Spirit guiding him, Paul chose to rise above his situation through trusting in God's will for him moment by moment. He chose to focus on what attitudes would uplift his spirit and glorify God. He learned it. This tells me that it took times of failure and times of success as God was teaching him to be content in whatever was happening in his life. Paul chose to be thankful.

We, too, can live a life of being content no matter if we have to live in a tent, or we are hungry having perhaps but a small potato to eat, or being persecuted, or going through a bankruptcy, or having lost a loved one, just to name a few. The *secret* of having this mindset is what Paul said in the verses above. I can choose to be content and grateful through Christ who empowers me to do so. Again, notice that Paul says *"he has learned"* to be content. Complaining is something that comes naturally to our human nature whereas being thankful is something that needs to be developed and practiced. It is a way of thinking. It is finding the good in the place where we are at instead of complaining and focusing on the negative.

In my own life, I have struggled to learn contentment and thankfulness in whatever state I find myself. I remember when Ike and I and Joseph our son enjoyed living in a nice little house in the desert area. We had a good life and we were truly blessed. Things changed though when Ike's elderly mother had to move in with us (as I previously mentioned) because she broke her neck. How happy would I be now? I was not happy. I did not want to be a caretaker. I had enough in my own daily life to deal with, but Mom was to stay with us for almost four years and I struggled the whole time. I not only had to constantly remind myself to live in my present so I could handle the daily pressures, but I had to work on my attitudes toward my mom-in-law. I worked on being grateful and thankful, and the next thing I knew I was confessing an impatient and a short-temper to God.

At times I thought that I had the victory because I felt some contentment in my circumstance, some peace and acceptance, but then something new would pop up. I was *learning* how to be thankful and content. Then, as I mentioned before, we moved to Orange County where Ike and I went back to school and we lived in a townhouse with our mom. After a while Mom moved into assisted living, for we could no longer take care of her. We then moved into an apartment which was so different than having our own house. People lived so close together, and there wasn't much privacy. We moved on to the third floor and everyone smoked cigarettes. The smoke would rise up into our apartment when the windows were open, but I was determined to find the positive aspects of where we lived.

I remember the night when I laid my head down on my pillow how thankful I was for the apartment. The days we lived in this apartment I began to really learn to be content for most of the time. I had a great sense of peace that God knew what He was presently doing in our lives and He would move us when He chose to. After we finished our Master's program we were ready for our next move. Little did I know that the hardest years of my life were yet to come, and all I had ever learned about being thankful I would have to draw upon. Meanwhile, I purposed in my little heart to be thankful and not to complain about my circumstances as we returned to another apartment in the desert.

We had only been in our place for a little over two years when the tragedy struck. Our 22 year old son was living with us at the time and going to junior college. It was a night I can never forget when the officer coroner came to our house to give us the news that our son had been hit by a car and he didn't make it. I go into detail all about this in my book, *From Ashes to Praise.* I do recall after the officer left I went downstairs to the garage and threw up my hands. I said, "The Lord gives and the Lord takes away. Blessed be the name of the Lord!" I purposed then and there to trust God completely over the death of my son. I trusted His goodness, His wisdom, His compassion, His purpose and His love in the matter. However, this was the beginning of more lessons to be learned and further master when it came to having a thankful heart.

I have to say that God has been so faithful to me during my intense years of mourning and grief. I would literally have to choose to say thank you to the Lord over and over through tears streaming down my cheeks for giving me the gift of my beautiful son. I would look for things to be thankful for and audibly applaud God for His blessings. God brought me through and I praise Him for this. I know though that this lesson of being thankful will be one I will always be working on as I encounter different seasons in my life.

Each day I want to wake up and go to bed thanking God for all I have been given. We all could make a list of what God has done in our lives? What He has blessed us with? We *can* be content when we appreciate what God has done for and with us and what He is doing now. Paul had the right mindset, and I want to have the same one.

And so how does a grateful heart make a troubled heart at peace? I believe that what we are thinking influences how we are feeling. If we are anxious and fearful our bodies and emotions will react and respond in this way. The answer is to think good thoughts as the Apostle Paul tells us in that same book when he was in prison. Philippians, chapter four says that we are to think on things that are *"true, whatever is noble, whatever is right, whatever is pure, whatever is lovely, whatever is admirable—if anything is excellent or praiseworthy—we are to think about such things."* God wants us to dwell on the positive things in life, and when we train our minds to think on what pleases God the end result will be peace for Paul goes on to say, *"put it into practice and the God of peace will be with you."*

For further study on having the right mind-set refer to my book, *Hope in a Season of Suffering*. We will continue on now to our fifth powerful step to happiness and that is to *always choose love.*

5

ALWAYS CHOOSE LOVE

THE BIBLE TALKS a lot about love. God loved us first as it says in 1 John, chapters 3-4. We are told that God has lavished His great love upon us that we should be called His children. He showed us His love by *"sending His only Son into the world that we might live through Him."* But even when we didn't love God, *"He loved us and sent His Son as an atoning sacrifice for our sins."* God *so loved* us, so we ought also to love God and others. The Bible plainly says *"God is love."* If we live in His love, His *"love will be made complete"* in us. It goes on to say that *"There is no fear in love but perfect love drives out fear, because fear has to do with punishment. We love because He first loved us."*

Clearly, the source of love is God, and we can love others because we are loved by God. However, even though we are truly loved by God it is not easy for some of us to internalize this love because of hurtful experiences we may have gone through in our lives.

Many of us have been wounded through the process of living and we need to learn to let love back into our hearts. Sometimes this means that we need to get some help from good counselors in order to take down the walls we have put up. And of course, it is wise to have a godly minister to pray over you that God would bring healing to those hurt places. I believe that it is completely possible to allow love back into our hearts to bring us healing, comfort and restoration.

I have had to work hard in allowing love to take deep root in my own heart. I had been wounded emotionally and had built up walls that would keep love out because of fear of being hurt again. (How many of us do that—let love come only so far and then shoot it down because of the fear of more pain?) In my sessions with my therapist I worked persistently hard learning to allow others to love and care about me. I also joined in group therapy where I learned to let love in when it presented itself.

What do I mean when I say this—letting love into our lives? I mean to say *yes* whenever genuine love presents itself. Example? When I was learning this truth I remember someone would compliment me on something and I would blow it off not completely receiving it as true. However, with practice, I allowed the compliments to sink into my heart. I gave myself permission to feel the joy that came along with them. I allowed the love to come in and melt away the walls of numbness. When someone would hug me I received it and hugged back. I even had to say to myself, "I receive love. I let this love and care into my heart—I allow myself to feel it."

I did this with God's love also. At first I felt so guilty and unworthy of His love that I would dodge thinking about it for any length of time. Finally, as I spiritually and emotionally matured, and went through different experiences I learned more about God's love. I worked on forgiving myself of my weaknesses, sins and failures and then received God's forgiveness for my sins. You see, I had not internalized this awesome truth of Jesus having forgiven me completely. Somewhere I thought I had to do some penance so I would become worthy. To grasp this great truth I spent many days going over and over the Scriptures that talk about God having forgiven us in Christ. I would meditate upon those verses until they became a part of my soul. I also would remind myself, on the days I felt lousy and unlovable, that God's Word was still true. Nothing changed. I was still washed in the blood of the Lamb, Jesus. All my shortcomings and failings had already been forgiven and God saw me covered in the righteousness of His Son. God still adored me being His child and doted over me. **Remember, that feelings and emotions come and go and change from day to day, but this has nothing to do with the truth of what God has**

said. Knowing this truth and believing it will keep you anchored in your faith on challenging days.

During the years God showed me His love in so many ways until I began to really get it deep down in my heart. I could be happy knowing that I was loved and accepted. I envisioned the Lord as a good heavenly Father embracing and loving me. I felt safe in His arms as I allowed myself to be cherished and cared for. It took practice. I had to change the way I saw the Father.

He was not angry with me, nor did He ever condemn me. He knew me perfectly and still loved me.

Now how do we choose love when it presents itself? And how does it present itself? Love presents itself in so many different ways. Some ways are: a kind word, a loving touch, a smile, a hug, giving a little gift, sending a card, being courteous, sharing something we have, listening, going out for lunch, walking together, giving a compliment, making something for someone—like popcorn to share, being patient, being helpful, these are just a few ways. And then instead of minimizing these as not important or necessary because we don't want to get close to anyone—we must take the risk and let love in.

Hang out with good people, safe and kind people. Don't allow yourself to be abused by anyone; respect yourself as you would another human being. Don't be afraid to open up to a safe person—again, take a risk. It is so worth it.

Finally, I would like to share some of my thoughts of when I was beginning to take these risks myself struggling to receive love into my life. I recorded these ideas and feelings in one of my very first books, *Honest Heart*. I Hope these devotional writings will help. Now I will close this chapter on "Always Choose Love" with these poetic writings.

Bonding

Oh God, this pain of mine hurts! Today I hurt especially bad. I am seeing how I really need to emotionally connect—I've been afraid of rejection.

But oh, God, I am ready now to pull down my walls and put down my defenses and to allow myself to be loved and to love. To allow myself to need another person and to show that very vulnerable need (that we all have as human beings). Oh God, I do need people—help me to allow myself to form deep and healthy bonds with safe people—to allow myself to be knit together with Your people in love, truth and grace.

Oh God, You have provided the means in which I can mend. Help me to grab hold of that human hand and move forward toward wholeness.

Oh, God, enable me to attach to some good people where I can truly feel loved and significant; where I can truly be myself and have a sense of belonging—where I can also give my love, affirmation and encouragement. Thank You Lord, for Your people… I am moving forward toward wholeness.

Scripture Reading: Ephesians 4:15-16

I Say Yes To Life

I love life, Lord. I love being alive. Taking risks in living means we are alive. Taking no risks keeps us stagnant. If we are not daily growing, we are coming to a standstill and we may be regressing. Lord, I love to live. Loving people is being alive. Caring, helping and working in my community is being alive. Having children and raising them is living. Working at marriage and relationships— working hard to understand and complement each other is really experiencing being alive.
Serving You, Lord, is abundant life. Knowing You is life itself. Help me to say yes to love every time it presents itself for in doing this I am saying yes to life.

Scripture Reading: John 10:10; Ecclesiastes 3:1-8

Dare I take A Risk?

Dare I take a risk Lord—show my vulnerable side?
Dare I take a risk—And share my deepest thoughts?
Dare I take a risk and display my very soul?
*Oh Lord, I could be rejected or ridiculed. I could
be thought less of as a person—or disregarded
and oh, I don't want to feel worthless and unloved
and unaccepted.*
*But what if I choose not to take the risk of sharing
with someone my true self, my inner self?*
I will then truly feel alienated and unloved.
*Lord, I want to take the risk of sharing, of revealing
myself to others…to people who are safe and can
give me grace. There are people I can trust Lord.*
*I can take the risk of becoming bonded with
others in Your kingdom.*
*I may experience pain and rejection but I know
I can also experience warmth and closeness and
healing from past rejections. And this is worth it!*
Lord, I'll take the risk. I'll take the risk.

**Scripture Reading: 1 Corinthians 13;
Philippians 4:13**

Someone Cares

Someone complimented me today.
She touched my hand—I feel alive!
Someone cares about me.

Someone wrote me a letter today.
She touched my heart—I was moved to tears—
she encouraged me and blessed me.
Lord, I feel good. Someone cares about me.

Someone prayed for me today.
And I felt Your presence with me in a closer way.
I had a little more strength for my day. I had a
lift of lightness in my step.

Someone smiled at me. My burdens seemed a little
easier to bear.
Lord, someone cares about me.

❧

Scripture Reading: 1 Peter 5:7; Proverbs 11:25

Today I Choose

Lord, as of today, I choose to really believe that I am loved—deeply loved by You. As of right now I accept the fact that I am cared for and wanted by You. Right this moment I rejoice and accept You loving me, forgiving me and cherishing me.

Today, I accept the security and warmth I have in You, Lord. You are my good Father. I rest in Your grace.

It feels good to be loved and to know I am watched over. It feels good to know I have You, Father God, and I can truly rely on Your goodness, love and understanding.

Lord, today I choose to love others.

❧

Scripture Reading: 1 John 4; Psalm 57:10-11

"Above all, clothe yourselves with love, which binds us all together in perfect harmony"(Colossians 3:14 NLT).

Now let's move on to the sixth step *of letting the Word of God transform your thinking.*

6

LET THE WORD OF GOD TRANSFORM YOUR THINKING

*T*HIS IS ONE of the most powerful, life-changing things you can do. You can do it every day, any time—day or night. God tells us to be transformed in our thinking as we have become born again into His kingdom and we are made new in our inner man, our spirit. Romans 12:2 says, *"Do not conform to the pattern of this world, but be transformed by the renewing of your mind. Then you will be able to test and approve what God's will is—His good, pleasing and perfect will."* I want to do God's will. I want to think like God thinks. The Bible also tells us that we have the mind of Christ (1 Corinthians 2:16). Wow! This means we can think the thoughts of God and be changed in our attitudes. This means we can experience more peace and more happiness in our lives.

Currently, God has me in an intense learning mode. I am becoming even more diligent and persistent to let God's words take pre-eminence in my thought life. If you can think right you can make it through any trial. If you can think right you can be happier. If you think right, you will be pleasing God more and you will love God, yourself, and others more. So how do we do this? How do we let the Word of God transform our thinking?

All of us have areas where we can be bombarded with fearful, doubtful, and destructive thoughts. Areas such as our self-esteem, security, relationships, values, beliefs, and opinions where change needs to take place. Change doesn't happen overnight but you have to start somewhere. So let's start at the beginning of the day, morning. I wake up and I wonder how I am feeling. Am I feeling good? Or am I feeling down under? Are my thoughts just wandering or do I have a purpose for where I want them to take me? Yes! I have a purpose. I want to be happy today! I want to accomplish something today. So I deliberately begin to feed into my mind some God-thoughts to get me going in the right direction. Some of the things I can say to myself are, "Today I can be happy. I really can. I can enjoy the life I have and be thankful for each and every little thing God has blessed me with. I can be happy because I am loved by God. I can be happy because my sins are all washed away. I can be happy because all of the Bible is true and therefore my faith can be real and work for me. I can be happy. I can have hope. Not only do I have the strength to make it through this day, but I have more than enough strength to face each moment of my day. My soul can be content because I am not alone. The Holy Spirit is with and in me. He is my constant Companion. He is my Comforter. I can have joy and dance because I have a future and a hope in God! I have a home in heaven and I am wrapped up in the righteousness of Christ in God! Today I will do what I can to serve God and others. Today I will be kinder and more thoughtful. Today I will enjoy the beauty of God's creation and nature. Lord, here I am, Your beloved daughter! Lead me—let's go forward."

Doesn't that sound pretty encouraging to wake up to? But how about if you wake up and you are feeling really low? Perhaps you have lost your job, or are going through a divorce, or your child is struggling with drugs and alcohol, or you have just been told the cancer has returned, or your mate is sick, or you've just lost someone you love. There are so many reasons why we might wake up feeling the heaviness of the world on our shoulders. What then? This is when the real work is done in transforming our mind to think like Jesus.

With your *will* that God has given you, you have to make some choices in what direction you want your day to take you. Sometimes it is a day that you need to just chill out and lie on the couch and watch a movie or read a book. Tell yourself it's okay. It's okay to grieve when you need to. It's okay to cry if you need to. It's okay to do nothing but just *be* if need be. But it is not okay to allow destructive thoughts to take over your thinking and grip your heart. Some destructive thoughts might be: *I feel awful and hopeless. I will never feel any better. Every day is a hard day for me and I can't stand it anymore. I am a failure. I feel so alone and no one understands what I am going through. I'm tired of hurting. I can't change. It's too hard. It's my fault this and that happened so now I carry a load of guilt. I am such a weakling. I am a victim of my circumstances.*

You must catch yourself when the thoughts and emotions come flying at you. Sit down if you must and begin to change what you are thinking. How do we do this? We think and talk like God would. We do not, however, mask the problem or pretend it doesn't exist, we acknowledge that we are out of sorts, we do hurt, we don't like it. The next thing to do is to take the matter that is distressing us to prayer. Very simply we ask God to help us with our problem. Give us wisdom to know what to do. Guide us and direct us to where we can get support and help. Then we place it, the best we can at this point, in the hands of God. We then are ready to feed the good into our hearts and minds. We can say something like this: " I'm feeling really bad this morning. My body really hurts and the pain is intense. But even though I feel this way, I have prayed about it and I choose to trust that God is working on my problem. I choose to open my Bible and find words that will fill me up with hope. I will write down some verses to carry with me throughout my day when I need to remind myself of the goodness of God. I will make it through this day with God's help. I hold on to my hope."

God desires that we train our thinking to reflect His Word. Therefore we need to know what His Word says and how we can apply it to our own lives. Some of my favorite verses that help me through a difficult day are as follows.

"What shall we say about such wonderful things as these? If God is for us, who can ever be against us" (Romans 8:31 NLT)?

Then applied to my situation: Because God is for me, I know He will give me favor with the people around me.

"When I am afraid, I put my trust in You. In God, whose word I praise— in God I trust and am not afraid. What can mere mortals do to me" (Psalm 56:3-4)?

Applied to my situation: When I think of my pain it makes me feel afraid. What if it gets worse? I choose to put my trust in You, God, when this fear arises. Your Word tells me not to be afraid because You are bigger and greater than anything I am facing or going through. You helped David to slay the giant Goliath in the Bible. You will help me to slay my Goliaths also. So, I choose to trust You to take care of me today.

"For the weapons of our warfare are not carnal but mighty in God for pulling down strongholds, casting down arguments and every high thing that exalts itself against the knowledge of God, bringing every thought into captivity to the obedience of Christ" (2 Corinthians 10:4-5 NKJV).

Applied to my situation: I am not fighting these battles by myself. God is with me and He has given me everything I need to make it through, moment by moment. Through the power of the Holy Spirit I can pull down those destructive thoughts that the devil throws at me and I can capture every thought that is contrary to what God says. I can choose to think on what is uplifting and life producing. Even if I have to do this daily, I will learn and master a new way of thinking. I want to live with having the mind of Christ.

"Christ gives me the strength to face anything" *(Philippians 4:13 Contemporary English Version).*

Applied to my situation: Today I have what I need to face anything that comes my way. I will not be shaken with bad news. My trust is in God. He says fear not for I am with you. Each moment I have strength to handle what's going on in my life. I can react and respond with calmness of heart and wisdom of mind. I can be brave. I am brave. I am courageous. I have made it this far, I will keep moving forward. God's plans for me are for good and to give me hope and a future. I trust Him with my life. He will never fail me.

Can you see what I am talking about? Saying what God says to you and about you. To do this you must get into the Bible. Get an easy to read Bible and begin to find verses that speak to your particular need. You can use the concordances that are at the very back pages of the Bible. Or look things up online. Plug in verses for not being afraid, or verses for strength, verses for hope and so forth. As you begin to build new thinking patterns, and this takes time and persistence, you will begin to feel more control of your life, more peace, and of course, this will make you feel happier. A transformed mind is a peaceful mind rather than a chaotic one. I want a peaceful mind.

Remember a note here: Keep up the good work even if you don't *feel* like it. Feelings have nothing to do with faith. Feelings can change from one moment to the next. Just keep steady. Keep focused. Transformation will happen as you implant God's Word. The Holy Spirit of God will activate His words to your spirit and mind to bring about change. Finally, the last powerful step to bringing happiness into your life is *to learn and understand who you are in Christ.*

7

LEARN AND UNDERSTAND WHO YOU ARE IN CHRIST

THIS IS THE last step to happiness. Knowing and grasping an understanding of who you are in Christ and about your new life will empower you even more to live a victorious Christian life. You see, when we become born again in our spirit something happens to us. Let me explain.

When we ask Jesus to come into our life, to forgive us of our sins and to send His Holy Spirit, a new birth takes place right in that second of believing and receiving the Savior. The grace of God gives us the faith we need to believe in God's free gift of eternal life, and we take the next move to receive this great gift, Jesus, Himself, into our life. When our faith unites with God's truth we become born again in our spirit man. Before we had Christ in our life, our spirit was dead to spiritual things. However, we were still living in our body with our soul, which is our intellect, emotions and will. We were walking around without God and our spirit was not alive. The Bible says, *"As for you, you were dead in your transgressions and sins" (Ephesians 2:1)*. Our sinful flesh and soulish man could not live for God or be acceptable to God, for God is holy. Our sinful flesh and soulish man cannot resist sin but succumbs to it. Sure we can do good things and be a nice person, but our spirit still is dead to the things of God. All our good deeds cannot give us a new heart, only God can do this.

At the moment we acknowledge our sin to God and ask for forgiveness, and we accept and believe that Jesus Christ, His Son, died on the cross for our sin and rose again so we could live, our spirit becomes reborn. The Word of God which comes to us, either spoken or written, when mixed with our faith brings regeneration to our spirit through God's Holy Spirit. We, at this point, are accepted by God, adopted as His child and placed into His kingdom. I know this is a lot of information I am giving you, but go back and reread if need be. Let these truths sink into your heart.

Here are some phrases the Bible uses in describing this new nature we are given as a believer in Christ.

New life in Christ.

Regeneration by the Holy Spirit.

Born again of incorruptible seed, the Word of God.

Raised in newness of life.

Passed from death into life.

Made alive.

Raised to sit in heavenly places in Christ.

A new creation.

New self, created in the likeness of God.

Old self, crucified with Christ.

Born of God.

Walk in newness of life.

We have the mind of Christ.

We have eternal life in Christ.

Christ lives in me.

In Christ I am made alive.

Therefore, having a new nature that is born of God, we have now the power to resist sin and obey God. We are to begin to live our new life and grow up into Him, that is, Jesus Christ. Our spirit man can grow stronger and mature as we feed upon the Word of God and talk to God in prayer. God's very life lives in us now and we have everything we need in order to live a godly life.

Are we perfect? No, not until we enter into heaven, but we are to grow more like Jesus daily. We are to put off the old man with his deeds and to put on the new man which is created in holiness.

Remember: It is important to realize that we have two natures now that battle against each other. We have the old nature of sin, that is in our flesh and soul, and the new nature in our spirit. Our soul, or our mind was not regenerated when we were born again. This is why we must be renewed in our mind. We must no longer be conformed to the old sinful lifestyle but to be transformed by the renewing of our mind. Remember I spoke about putting the Word of God in our thoughts and allowing it to rule our lives? There will be a struggle between the old and the new. So we train our mind to think along the same lines as our new nature. This is called "sanctification." This is a process that we will undergo throughout our entire life time.

Now when God looks at us, He no longer sees sin and shame, but He sees us in Christ wrapped up in His righteousness and justified from all our trespasses and sins. What do we do if we sin now? We agree with God that we missed it and get back on track. God says that He will forgive us and cleanse us from all our sins by the blood of His Son, Jesus. Let's take a look now at how the old man and his mindset thinks and the new man with his mindset.

Before I became born again I lived according to my flesh. I was dominated by my fleshly desires. I lived the life of sinful behavior apart from God. I tried many times to turn over a new leaf and "be good" but that lasted for a few days and I was back at my old stuff again, feeling guilty and powerless. When I received my new nature and my spirit man was made alive, I could now resist the sins that I once was daily caught up in, and I could choose to go God's way. However, my mind had to be renewed and this is where the real work is done and where the battle is fought—good over evil. It took me many years to understand the victory God had given me and wanted me to receive and walk in. It doesn't have to take you that long if you understand who you are in Christ, now as a child of God, with the power of His Holy Spirit living in you.

There was so much I didn't know at the time. God began to teach me. As I had mentioned before, I had experienced a mental break down at the age of seventeen, and the chemistry in my brain had been altered by all the intense stress I was experiencing. The *feel good* chemicals that our brains have, such as serotonin and endorphins, were not functioning the way they should have. Because of this, I suffered a great deal of agony. Fear, panic and guilt were daily emotions for me for many years. When I would ask God to forgive me I never felt forgiven. Fear would control me in certain stressful situations. How could I overcome and live this victorious life that God had for me? I prayed and studied God's Word. I listened to pastors and teachers and grasped at what morsels of truth that could set me free. I did not understand that Christ had already set me free. I did not understand that where the Spirit of the Lord is there is liberty. I needed healing in my emotions.

As God continued to teach me His truths, my spiritual eyes became opened to the degree where the Word of God began to really change my thinking patterns. I was being transformed by the renewing of my mind. I began to see the truth more clearly.

The old nature doubts. The new nature believes.

The old nature fears. The new nature has faith.

The old nature feels guilty. The new nature has no condemnation.

The old nature feels victim mentality. The new nature has power over all the power of the enemy and can do what God says it can.

The old nature is moody and crabby. The new nature chooses to put on Christ and to cultivate a heart of thanksgiving and gratitude.

The old nature holds resentments. The new nature forgives.

The old nature gets overwhelmed and out of control.

The new nature chooses to trust in the direction and will of God.

The old nature thinks of itself better than others. The new nature cultivates the heart of humility.

The old nature complains and murmurs. The new nature learns to be content in whatever state it finds itself.

You get the picture! You are a new person in Christ. You have a new nature. The old nature, although it dwells in your flesh, does not have to dominate you. You can choose to be led by the Spirit. Being led by the Spirit of God will bring you, life and peace. You will be a happy soul. The Bible says *"Happy is that people, that is in such a case: yea, happy is that people, whose God is the LORD"* (Psalm 144:15).

So how do I do this? Walk and be led by the Holy Spirit? Be an overcomer? Overcome sin and bondages? This is a daily plan. This is a daily work. This is a daily walk. I will say this, that the more we digest and allow the Word of God to dominate our life the more victory we will begin to experience. It is making choices every day, sometimes each moment of the day. It's saying, "No. I don't want to think that way. I want to think God's way. No. I don't want to be dominated by that fear, the Bible says I am free and so I choose to thank God for breaking the yoke of fear and giving me liberty in my thinking. No. I don't want to respond to that person with ugliness in my heart. I choose love. I choose kindness. I choose to think of others rather than just focus on myself. No. I won't go there in my mind. I won't go where destructive thoughts want to lead me. I won't be led by them. Rather I will let the Word of God lead me. God has not given me the spirit that cringes in fear, but He has given me the spirit that loves people, loves God, and myself. He has given me the spirit that is powerful in overcoming wrongful and hurtful ways of living and thinking. He has also given me a mind that thinks logically and is balanced. I can reason and think with wisdom, understanding, and knowledge."

You see, this transformation that takes place in us depends upon our dependence upon God's Spirit who lives in us. We must go to Him and talk to Him about everything and ask Him for His help to overcome areas where we are struggling. When we become wrapped up in loving the Savior and receiving His love for us…we are being transformed. The more time we spend with Him getting to know Him and learning of Him, the more we can live victorious in a world that holds uncertainty and constant change. Always choose God. Always choose love. Always choose what is good.

CONCLUSION

THESE SEVEN POWERFUL steps to happiness have become a huge part of my life that I daily practice. Some seasons in my life I focus more on one of the steps than on another as God is working with me. It is a wonderful, challenging, stretching, life-filled journey that we walk when we follow these steps to life and happiness. I pray that God will empower you to put into practice these principles and that you will feel a new hope and peace in your life as you move forward.

And when the practicing gets hard or uncomfortable keep on plugging away because the Bible says, *"all hard work will bring about a profit."* What you sow into your life you will also reap. The benefits outweigh the difficult moments and we can tolerate anything for the higher gain—that of being at peace and being happy with God, ourselves, people and life itself. God bless you. I am cheering for you as you work on living life to its fullest.